Due Return	Due Return
Date Date	Date Date

HELMETS

HELMETS

POEMS BY

James Dickey

Wesleyan University Press
MIDDLETOWN, CONNECTICUT

Most of these poems have been previously published elsewhere. For permission to reprint them in this volume, the author is grateful to the editors of *Hudson Review; The Paris Review; The Sewanee Review; The Virginia Quarterly Review; The Yale Review; The New Yorker*, in which the following first appeared: "At Darien Bridge," "The Beholders," "Breath," "Bums, on Waking," "Cherrylog Road," "The Driver," "The Dusk of Horses," "Fence Wire," "Goodbye to Serpents," "The Ice Skin," "Kudzu," "In the Marble Quarry," "The Poisoned Man," "The Scarred Girl," and Part I of "On the Coosawattee"; and *Poetry*, in which the following first appeared: "The Being," "A Folk Singer of the Thirties," and Part II of "On the Coosawattee."

I should like to thank the editors of *The Virginia Quarterly Review* for the Emily Balch Prize awarded to "Springer Mountain," and the directors of the John Simon Guggenheim Memorial Foundation for the fellowship on which these poems were written.

Library of Congress Catalog Card Number : 64-13610
Manufactured in the United States of America
*First printing February 1964; second printing January 1966;
third printing October 1966; fourth printing December 1967*

To Maxine

light and warmth

CONTENTS

PART ONE

THE DUSK OF HORSES

Right under their noses, the green
Of the field is paling away
Because of something fallen from the sky.

They see this, and put down
Their long heads deeper in grass
That only just escapes reflecting them

As the dream of a millpond would.
The color green flees over the grass
Like an insect, following the red sun over

The next hill. The grass is white.
There is no cloud so dark and white at once;
There is no pool at dawn that deepens

Their faces and thirsts as this does.
Now they are feeding on solid
Cloud, and, one by one,

With nails as silent as stars among the wood
Hewed down years ago and now rotten,
The stalls are put up around them.

Now if they lean, they come
On wood on any side. Not touching it, they sleep.
No beast ever lived who understood

What happened among the sun's fields,
Or cared why the color of grass
Fled over the hill while he stumbled,

Led by the halter to sleep
On his four taxed, worthy legs.
Each thinks he awakens where

The sun is black on the rooftop,
That the green is dancing in the next pasture,
And that the way to sleep

In a cloud, or in a risen lake,
Is to walk as though he were still
In the drained field standing, head down,

To pretend to sleep when led,
And thus to go under the ancient white
Of the meadow, as green goes

And whiteness comes up through his face
Holding stars and rotten rafters,
Quiet, fragrant, and relieved.

FENCE WIRE

Too tight, it is running over
Too much of this ground to be still
Or to do anything but tremble
And disappear left and right
As far as the eye can see

Over hills, through woods,
Down roads, to arrive at last
Again where it connects,
Coming back from the other side
Of animals, defining their earthly estate

As the grass becomes snow
While they are standing and dreaming
Of grass and snow.
The winter hawk that sits upon its post,
Feeling the airy current of the wires,

Turns into a robin, sees that this is wrong,
Then into a boy, and into a man who holds
His palm on the top tense strand
With the whole farm feeding slowly
And nervously into his hand.

If the wire were cut anywhere
All his blood would fall to the ground
And leave him standing and staring
With a face as white as a Hereford's.
From years of surrounding grain,

Cows, horses, machinery trying to turn
To rust, the humming arrives each second,
A sound that arranges these acres
And holds them highstrung and enthralled.
Because of the light, chilled hand

On the top thread tuned to an E
Like the low string of a guitar,
The dead corn is more
Balanced in death than it was,
The animals more aware

Within the huge human embrace
Held up and borne out of sight
Upon short, unbreakable poles
Wherethrough the ruled land intones
Like a psalm: properly,

With its eyes closed,
Whether on the side of the animals
Or not, whether disappearing
Right, left, through trees or down roads,
Whether outside, around, or in.

AT DARIEN BRIDGE

The sea here used to look
As if many convicts had built it,

Standing deep in their ankle chains,
Ankle-deep in the water, to smite

The land and break it down to salt.
I was in this bog as a child

When they were all working all day
To drive the pilings down.

I thought I saw the still sun
Strike the side of a hammer in flight

And from it a sea bird be born
To take off over the marshes.

As the gray climbs the side of my head
And cuts my brain off from the world,

I walk and wish mainly for birds,
For the one bird no one has looked for

To spring again from a flash
Of metal, perhaps from the scratched

Wedding band on my ring finger.
Recalling the chains of their feet,

I stand and look out over grasses
At the bridge they built, long abandoned,

Breaking down into water at last,
And long, like them, for freedom

Or death, or to believe again
That they worked on the ocean to give it

The unchanging, hopeless look
Out of which all miracles leap.

CHENILLE

There are two facing peacocks
     Or a ship flapping
On its own white tufted sail
At roadside, near a mill;

Flamingoes also are hanging
     By their bills on bedspreads
And an occasional mallard.
These you can buy anywhere.
They are made by machine
From a sanctioned, unholy pattern
Rigid with industry.
They hoard the smell of oil

And hum like looms all night
     Into your pores, reweaving
Your body from bobbins.
There is only one quiet

Place — in a scuppernong arbor —
     Where animals as they
Would be, are born into sleep-cloth:
A middle-aged man's grandmother
Sits in the summer green light
Of leaves, gone toothless
For eating grapes better,
And pulls the animals through

With a darning needle:
     Deer, rabbits and birds,
Red whales and unicorns,
Winged elephants, crowned ants:

Beasts that cannot be thought of
    By the wholly sane
Rise up in the rough, blurred
Flowers of fuzzy cloth
In only their timeless outlines
Like the beasts of Heaven:
Those sketched out badly, divinely
By stars not wholly sane.

Love, I have slept in that house.
    There it was winter.
The tattered moonfields crept
Through the trellis, and fell

In vine-tangled shade on my face
    Like thrown-away knitting
Before cloud came and dimmed
Those scars from off me.
My fingernails chilled
To the bone. I called
For another body to be
With me, and warm us both.

A unicorn neighed; I folded
    His neck in my arms
And was safe, as he lay down.
All night, from thickening Heaven,

Someone up there kept throwing
    Bedspreads upon me.
Softly I called, and they came:
The ox and the basilisk,   ·

The griffin, the phoenix, the lion —
Light-bodied, only the essence,
The tufted, creative starfields
Behind the assembling clouds —

The snake from the apple tree came
        To save me from freezing,
And at last the lung-winged ship
On its own sail scented with potash

Fell sighing upon us all.
        The last two nails
Of cold died out in my nostrils
Under the dance-weight of beasts.
I lay, breathing like thread,
An inspired outline of myself,
As rain began greatly to fall,
And closed the door of the Ark.

ON THE COOSAWATTEE

1. By Canoe Through the Fir Forest

Into the slain tons of needles,
On something like time and dark knowledge
That cannot be told, we are riding
Over white stones forward through fir trees,
To follow whatever the river
Through the clasping of roots follows deeply.

As we go inward, more trunks
Climb from the edge of the water
And turn on the banks and stand growing.
The nerves in the patches of tree-light
On the ripples can feel no death,
But shake like the wings of angels

With light hard-pressed to keep up
Though it is in place on each feather.
Heavy woods in one movement around us
Flow back along either side
Bringing in more essential curves;
Small stones in their thousands turn corners

Under water and bear us on
Through the glittering, surfacing wingbeats
Cast from above. As we pass over,
As we pass through each hover of gold,
We lift up our blades from the water
And the blades of our shoulders,

Our rowing-muscles, our wings,
Are still and tremble, undying,

Drifting deeper into the forest.
Each light comes into our life
Past the man in front's changed hair
Then along the wing-balancing floor

And then onto me and one eye
And into my mouth for an instant.
The stones beneath us grow rounder
As I taste the fretted light fall
Through living needles to be here
Like a word I can feed on forever

Or believe like a vision I have
Or want to conceive out of greenness.
While the world fades, it is *becoming*.
As the trees shut away all seeing,
In my mouth I mix it with sunlight.
Here, in the dark, it is *being*.

II. *Below Ellijay*

Coming into Ellijay on the green
Idling freeway of the broad river
From the hill farms and pine woods,
We saw first the little stores
That backed down the red clay banks,
The blue flash of bottleglass
And the rippled tin heat haze of sheds

Where country mechanics were frying.
A poultry-processing plant
Smoked in the late morning air;

The bridge we rode under clattered
As we wound back out into fields.
But the water that held us had changed;
The town had slowed it and used it;

The wind had died in the tool sheds.
When we looked overboard, we knew.
Each thing was mistakenly feathered,
Muffled thickly in cast-off whiteness:
Each log was bedraggled in plumage
And accepting more feathers from water;
Each boulder under the green

Was becoming a lewd, setting hen
Moultingly under us brooding
In the sick, buried wind of the river,
Wavering, dying, increasing
From the plucked refuse of the plant,
And beside us uselessly floated —
Following, dipping, returning,

Turning frankly around to eye us,
To eye something else, to eye
Us again — a skinned chicken head,
Its gaze unperturbed and abiding.
All morning we floated on feathers
Among the drawn heads which appeared
Everywhere, from under the logs

Of feathers, from upstream behind us,
Lounging back to us from ahead,
Until we believed ourselves doomed
And the planet corrupted forever,

With stones turned to pullets, not struggling
But into more monstrousness shed,
Our canoe trailing more and more feathers

And the eye of the devil upon us
Closing drunkenly in from all sides,
And could have been on the Styx
In the blaze of noon, till we felt
The quickening pulse of the rapids
And entered upon it like men
Who sense that the world can be cleansed

Among rocks pallid only with water,
And plunged there like the unborn
Who see earthly streams without taint
Flow beneath them, while their wing feathers
Slough off behind them in Heaven
As they dress in the blinding clothes
Of nakedness for their fall.

III. *The Inundation*

Down there is a stone that holds my deepest sleep
And buries it deeper and deeper
Under the green, skinny lake
That is going back into the Georgia hills
And climbing them day and night
Behind the new dam.

And there is another stone, that boiled with white,
Where Braselton and I clung and fought
With our own canoe

That flung us in the rapids we had ridden
So that it might turn and take on
A ton of mountain water

And swing and bear down through the flying cloud
Of foam upon our violent rock
And pin us there.
With our backs to the wall of that boulder,
We yelled and kept it off us as we could,
Broke both paddles,

Then wedged it with the paddle stumps up over
The rock till the hull split, and it leapt and fell
Into the afterfall.
In life preservers we whirled ourselves away
And floated aimlessly down into calm water,
Turning like objects,

Then crawled upon shore and were found in the afternoon
By Lucas Gentry and his hunting dog, asleep
On a vast, gentle stone.
At a touch we woke, and followed the strange woods boy
Up the bluff, looking down on the roaring river's
Last day in its bed.

And now I cannot sleep at all, until I think
Of the Coosa, out of a clear blue sky
Overswelling its banks,
Its great stones falling through it into dark,
Its creeks becoming inlets, where water
Skiers already poise.

Over me it rises, too, but breathable, like cloud,
A green and silver cloud above which quiet
Lucas Gentry stands.
His dog whines, as the last rock of the wild river
Goes under, its white water lapses green,
And the leaping stone

Where we almost died takes on the settled repose
Of that other where we lay down and met
Our profoundest sleep
Rising from it to us, as the battered sides
Of the canoe gave deeper and deeper shade,
And Lucas Gentry,

Who may have been the accepting spirit of the place
Come to call us to higher ground,
Bent to raise
Us from the sleep of the yet-to-be-drowned,
There, with the black dream of the dead canoe
Over our faces.

WINTER TROUT

In the concrete cells of the hatchery
He nourished a dream of living
Under the ice, the long preparations
For the strange heat of feeling slowly

Roofs melt to a rhythmic green,
But now, in the first cold of freedom,
Riding motionless under the road
Of ice, shaping the heart

Of the buried stream with his tail,
He knows that his powers come
From the fire and stillness of freezing.
With the small tremors of his form

The banks shift imperceptibly,
Shift back, tremble, settle,
Shift, all within utter stillness.
I keep in my quiver now

An arrow whose head is half-missing.
It is useless, but I will not change
The pulled, broken tooth of its head
For I have walked upon banks

Shaken with the watchfulness of trout
Like walking barefoot in sleep
On the swaying tips of a grainfield,
On the long, just-bending stems,

Almost weightless, able to leap
Great distances, yet not leaping
Because each step on that ground
Gave a new sense of limitless hope.

Under the ice the trout rode,
Trembling, in the mastered heart
Of the creek, with what he could do.
I set myself up as a statue

With a bow, my red woolen back
Climbed slowly by thoughtful brambles
And dead beggar-lice, to shoot
At an angle down through the shadow

Of ice, and spear the trout
With a shot like Ulysses'
Through the ax heads, with the great weapon.
I shot, and the trout did not move

But was gone, and the banks
Went rigid under my feet
As the arrow floated away
Under the paving of ice.

I froze my right hand to retrieve it
As a blessing or warning,
As a sign of the penalties
For breaking into closed worlds

Where the wary controllers lie
At the heart of their power,
A pure void of shadowy purpose
Where the gods live, attuning the world,

Laying plans for the first green
They ever have lived, to melt
The ice from their great crowns.
Their secret enemies break

Like statues, as the king rises slowly,
Keeping only the thinnest film
Of his element — imagination —
Before his eyes as he lifts

Into spring, with the wood upside down
Balanced perfectly in all its leaves
And roots as he deeply has
All winter made provision for,

The surface full of gold flakes
Of the raw undersides of leaves,
And the thing seen right,
For once, that winter bought.

SPRINGER MOUNTAIN

Four sweaters are woven upon me,
All black, all sweating and waiting,
And a sheepherder's coat's wool hood,
Buttoned strainingly, holds my eyes
With their sight deepfrozen outside them
From their gaze toward a single tree.
I am here where I never have been,
In the limbs of my warmest clothes,
Waiting for light to crawl, weakly
From leaf to dead leaf onto leaf
Down the western side of the mountain.
Deer sleeping in light far above me

Have already woken, and moved,
In step with the sun moving strangely
Down toward the dark knit of my thicket
Where my breath takes shape on the air
Like a white helmet come from the lungs.
The one tree I hope for goes inward
And reaches the limbs of its gold.
My eyesight hangs partly between
Two twigs on the upslanting ground,
Then steps like a god from the dead
Wet of a half-rotted oak log
Steeply into the full of my brow.
My thighbones groaningly break

Upward, releasing my body
To climb, and to find among humus
New insteps made of snapped sticks.
On my back the faggot of arrows
Rattles and scratches its feathers.

I go up over logs slowly
On my painfully reborn legs,
My ears putting out vast hearing
Among the invisible animals,

Passing under thin branches held still,
Kept formed all night as they were
By the thought of predictable light.
The sun comes openly in
To my mouth, and is blown out white,

But no deer is anywhere near me.
I sit down and wait as in darkness.

The sweat goes dead at the roots

Of my hair: a deer is created
Descending, then standing and looking.
The sun stands and waits for his horns

To move. I may be there, also,
Between them, in head bones uplifted
Like a man in an animal tree
Nailed until light comes:
A dream of the unfeared hunter
Who has formed in his brain in the dark
And rose with light into his horns,
Naked, and I have turned younger

At forty than I ever have been.
I hang my longbow on a branch.

The buck leaps away and then stops,
And I step forward, stepping out

Of my shadow and pulling over
My head one dark heavy sweater
After another, my dungarees falling
Till they can be kicked away,
Boots, socks, all that is on me
Off. The world catches fire.
I put an unbearable light
Into breath skinned alive of its garments:
I think, beginning with laurel,
Like a beast loving
With the whole god bone of his horns:
The green of excess is upon me
Like deer in fir thickets in winter
Stamping and dreaming of men
Who will kneel with them naked to break
The ice from streams with their faces
And drink from the lifespring of beasts.
He is moving. I am with him

Down the shuddering hillside moving
Through trees and around, inside
And out of stumps and groves
Of laurel and slash pine,
Through hip-searing branches and thorn
Brakes, unprotected and sure,
Winding down to the waters of life

Where they stand petrified in a creek bed
Yet melt and flow from the hills
At the touch of an animal visage,

Rejoicing wherever I come to
With the gold of my breast unwrapped,
My crazed laughter pure as good church-cloth,
My brain dazed and pointed with trying
To grow horns, glad that it cannot,
For a few steps deep in the dance
Of what I most am and should be
And can be only once in this life.
He is gone below, and I limp
To look for my clothes in the world,

A middle-aged, softening man
Grinning and shaking his head
In amazement to last him forever.
I put on the warm-bodied wool,
The four sweaters inside out,
The bootlaces dangling and tripping,
Then pick my tense bow off the limb
And turn with the unwinding hooftracks,
In my good, tricked clothes,
To hunt, under Springer Mountain,
Deer for the first and last time.

PART TWO

CHERRYLOG ROAD

Off Highway 106
At Cherrylog Road I entered
The '34 Ford without wheels,
Smothered in kudzu,
With a seat pulled out to run
Corn whiskey down from the hills,

And then from the other side
Crept into an Essex
With a rumble seat of red leather
And then out again, aboard
A blue Chevrolet, releasing
The rust from its other color,

Reared up on three building blocks.
None had the same body heat;
I changed with them inward, toward
The weedy heart of the junkyard,
For I knew that Doris Holbrook
Would escape from her father at noon

31

And would come from the farm
To seek parts owned by the sun
Among the abandoned chassis,
Sitting in each in turn
As I did, leaning forward
As in a wild stock-car race

In the parking lot of the dead.
Time after time, I climbed in
And out the other side, like
An envoy or movie star
Met at the station by crickets.
A radiator cap raised its head,

Become a real toad or a kingsnake
As I neared the hub of the yard,
Passing through many states,
Many lives, to reach
Some grandmother's long Pierce-Arrow
Sending platters of blindness forth

From its nickel hubcaps
And spilling its tender upholstery
On sleepy roaches,
The glass panel in between
Lady and colored driver
Not all the way broken out,

The back-seat phone
Still on its hook.
I got in as though to exclaim,
"Let us go to the orphan asylum,

John; I have some old toys
For children who say their prayers."

I popped with sweat as I thought
I heard Doris Holbrook scrape
Like a mouse in the southern-state sun
That was eating the paint in blisters
From a hundred car tops and hoods.
She was tapping like code,

Loosening the screws,
Carrying off headlights,
Sparkplugs, bumpers,
Cracked mirrors and gear-knobs,
Getting ready, already,
To go back with something to show

Other than her lips' new trembling
I would hold to me soon, soon,
Where I sat in the ripped back seat
Talking over the interphone,
Praying for Doris Holbrook
To come from her father's farm

And to get back there
With no trace of me on her face
To be seen by her red-haired father
Who would change, in the squalling barn,
Her back's pale skin with a strop,
Then lay for me

In a bootlegger's roasting car
With a string-triggered 12-gauge shotgun
To blast the breath from the air.
Not cut by the jagged windshields,
Through the acres of wrecks she came
With a wrench in her hand,

Through dust where the blacksnake dies
Of boredom, and the beetle knows
The compost has no more life.
Someone outside would have seen
The oldest car's door inexplicably
Close from within:

I held her and held her and held her,
Convoyed at terrific speed
By the stalled, dreaming traffic around us,
So the blacksnake, stiff
With inaction, curved back
Into life, and hunted the mouse

With deadly overexcitement,
The beetles reclaimed their field
As we clung, glued together,
With the hooks of the seat springs
Working through to catch us red-handed
Amidst the gray, breathless batting

That burst from the seat at our backs.
We left by separate doors
Into the changed, other bodies
Of cars, she down Cherrylog Road

And I to my motorcycle
Parked like the soul of the junkyard

Restored, a bicycle fleshed
With power, and tore off
Up Highway 106, continually
Drunk on the wind in my mouth,
Wringing the handlebar for speed,
Wild to be wreckage forever.

THE SCARRED GIRL

All glass may yet be whole
She thinks, it may be put together
From the deep inner flashing of her face.
One moment the windshield held

The countryside, the green
Level fields and the animals,
And these must be restored
To what they were when her brow

Broke into them for nothing, and began
Its sparkling under the gauze.
Though the still, small war for her beauty
Is stitched out of sight and lost,

It is not this field that she thinks of.
It is that her face, buried
And held up inside the slow scars,
Knows how the bright, fractured world

Burns and pulls and weeps
To come together again.
The green meadow lying in fragments
Under the splintered sunlight,

The cattle broken in pieces
By her useless, painful intrusion
Know that her visage contains
The process and hurt of their healing,

The hidden wounds that can
Restore anything, bringing the glass

Of the world together once more,
All as it was when she struck,

All except her. The shattered field
Where they dragged the telescoped car
Off to be pounded to scrap
Waits for her to get up,

For her calm, unimagined face
To emerge from the yards of its wrapping,
Red, raw, mixed-looking but entire,
A new face, an old life,

To confront the pale glass it has dreamed
Made whole and backed with wise silver,
Held in other hands brittle with dread,
A doctor's, a lip-biting nurse's,

Who do not see what she sees
Behind her odd face in the mirror:
The pastures of earth and of heaven
Restored and undamaged, the cattle

Risen out of their jagged graves
To walk in the seamless sunlight
And a newborn countenance
Put upon everything,

Her beauty gone, but to hover
Near for the rest of her life,
And good no nearer, but plainly
In sight, and the only way.

KUDZU

Japan invades. Far Eastern vines
Run from the clay banks they are

Supposed to keep from eroding,
Up telephone poles,
Which rear, half out of leafage,
As though they would shriek,
Like things smothered by their own
Green, mindless, unkillable ghosts.
In Georgia, the legend says
That you must close your windows

At night to keep it out of the house.
The glass is tinged with green, even so,

As the tendrils crawl over the fields.
The night the kudzu has
Your pasture, you sleep like the dead.
Silence has grown Oriental
And you cannot step upon ground:
Your leg plunges somewhere
It should not, it never should be,
Disappears, and waits to be struck

Anywhere between sole and kneecap:
For when the kudzu comes,

The snakes do, and weave themselves
Among its lengthening vines,
Their spade heads resting on leaves,
Growing also, in earthly power
And the huge circumstance of concealment.

One by one the cows stumble in,
Drooling a hot green froth,
And die, seeing the wood of their stalls

Strain to break into leaf.
In your closed house, with the vine

Tapping your window like lightning,
You remember what tactics to use.
In the wrong yellow fog-light of dawn
You herd them in, the hogs,
Head down in their hairy fat,
The meaty troops, to the pasture.
The leaves of the kudzu quake
With the serpents' fear, inside

The meadow ringed with men
Holding sticks, on the country roads.

The hogs disappear in the leaves.
The sound is intense, subhuman,
Nearly human with purposive rage.
There is no terror
Sound from the snakes.
No one can see the desperate, futile
Striking under the leaf heads.
Now and then, the flash of a long

Living vine, a cold belly,
Leaps up, torn apart, then falls

Under the tussling surface.
You have won, and wait for frost,
When, at the merest touch
Of cold, the kudzu turns
Black, withers inward and dies,
Leaving a mass of brown strings
Like the wires of a gigantic switchboard.
You open your windows,

With the lightning restored to the sky
And no leaves rising to bury

You alive inside your frail house,
And you think, in the opened cold,
Of the surface of things and its terrors,
And of the mistaken, mortal
Arrogance of the snakes
As the vines, growing insanely, sent
Great powers into their bodies
And the freedom to strike without warning:

From them, though they killed
Your cattle, such energy also flowed

To you from the knee-high meadow
(It was as though you had
A green sword twined among
The veins of your growing right arm —
Such strength as you would not believe
If you stood alone in a proper
Shaved field among your safe cows—):
Came in through your closed

Leafy windows and almighty sleep
And prospered, till rooted out.

THE BEHOLDERS

Far away under us, they are mowing on the green steps
Of the valley, taking long, unending swings
Among the ripe wheat.
It is something about them growing,
Growing smaller, that makes us look up and see
That what has come over them is a storm.

It is a blue-black storm the shape of this valley,
And includes, perhaps, in its darkness,
Three men in the air
Taking long, limber swings, cutting water.
Swaths start to fall and, on earth,
The men come closer together as they mow.

Now in the last stand of wheat they bend.
From above, we watch over them like gods,
Our chins on our hands,
Our great eyes staring, our throats dry
And aching to cry down on their heads
Some curse or blessing,

Some word we have never known, but we feel
That when the right time arrives, and more stillness,
Lightning will leap
From our mouths in reasonless justice
As they arc their scythes more slowly, taking care
Not to look up.

As darkness increases there comes
A dancing into each of their swings,
A dancing like men in a cloud.
We two are coming together

Also, along the wall.
No lightning yet falls from us

Where their long hooks catch on the last of the sun
And the color of the wheat passes upward,
Drawn off like standing water
Into the cloud, turning green;
The field becomes whiter and darker,
And fire in us gathers and gathers

Not to call down death to touch brightly
The only metal for miles
In the hands of judged, innocent men,
But for our use only, who in the first sheaves of rain
Sit thunderstruck, having now the power to speak
With deadly intent of love.

THE POISONED MAN

When the rattlesnake bit, I lay
In a dream of the country, and dreamed
Day after day of the river,

Where I sat with a jackknife and quickly
Opened my sole to the water.
Blood shed for the sake of one's life

Takes on the hid shape of the channel,
Disappearing under logs and through boulders.
The freezing river poured on

And, as it took hold of my blood,
Leapt up round the rocks and boiled over.
I felt that my heart's blood could flow

Unendingly out of the mountain,
Splitting bedrock apart upon redness,
And the current of life at my instep

Give deathlessly as a spring.
Some leaves fell from trees and whirled under.
I saw my struck bloodstream assume,

Inside the cold path of the river,
The inmost routes of a serpent
Through grass, through branches and leaves.

When I rose, the live oaks were ashen
And the wild grass was dead without flame.
Through the blasted cornfield I hobbled,

My foot tied up in my shirt,
And met my old wife in the garden,
Where she reached for a withering apple.

I lay in the country and dreamed
Of the substance and course of the river
While the different colors of fever

Like quilt patches flickered upon me.
At last I arose, with the poison
Gone out of the seam of the scar,

And brought my wife eastward and weeping,
Through the copper fields springing alive
With the promise of harvest for no one.

IN THE MARBLE QUARRY

Beginning to dangle beneath
The wind that blows from the undermined wood,
   I feel the great pulley grind,

The thread I cling to lengthen
And let me soaring and spinning down into marble,
   Hooked and weightlessly happy

Where the squared sun shines
Back equally from all four sides, out of stone
   And years of dazzling labor,

To land at last among men
Who cut with power saws a Parian whiteness
   And, chewing slow tobacco,

Their eyebrows like frost,
Shunt house-sized blocks and lash them to cables
   And send them heavenward

Into small-town banks,
Into the columns and statues of government buildings,
   But mostly graves.

I mount my monument and rise
Slowly and spinningly from the white-gloved men
   Toward the hewn sky

Out of the basement of light,
Sadly, lifted through time's blinding layers
   On perhaps my tombstone

In which the original shape
Michelangelo believed was in every rock upon earth
    Is heavily stirring,

    Surprised to be an angel,
To be waked in North Georgia by the ponderous play
    Of men with ten-ton blocks

    But no more surprised than I
To feel sadness fall off as though I myself
    Were rising from stone

    Held by a thread in midair,
Badly cut, local-looking, and totally uninspired,
    Not a masterwork

    Or even worth seeing at all
But the spirit of this place just the same,
    Felt here as joy.

A FOLK SINGER OF THE THIRTIES

On a bed of gravel moving
Over the other gravel
Roadbed between the rails, I lay
As in my apartment now.
I felt the engine enter
A tunnel a half-mile away
And settled deeper
Into the stones of my sleep
Drifting through North Dakota.
I pulled them over me
For warmth, though it was summer,
And in the dark we pulled

Into the freight yards of Bismarck.
In the gravel car buried
To my nose in sledge-hammered stones,
My guitar beside me straining
Its breast beneath the rock,
I lay in the buzzing yards
And crimson hands swinging lights
Saw my closed eyes burn
Open and shine in their lanterns.
The yard bulls pulled me out,
Raining a rockslide of pebbles.
Bashed in the head, I lay

On the ground
As in my apartment now.
I spat out my teeth
Like corn, as they jerked me upright
To be an example for
The boys who would ride the freights

Looking for work, or for
Their American lives.
Four held me stretching against
The chalked red boards,
Spreading my hands and feet,
And nailed me to the boxcar
With twenty-penny nails.
I hung there open-mouthed
As though I had no more weight
Or voice. The train moved out.

Through the landscape I edged
And drifted, my head on my breast
As in my clean sheets now,
And went flying sideways through
The country, the rivers falling
Away beneath my safe
Immovable feet,
Close to me as they fell
Down under the boiling trestles,
And the fields and woods
Unfolded. Sometimes, behind me,
Going into the curves,
Cattle cried in unison,
Singing of stockyards
Where their tilted blood
Would be calmed and spilled.
I heard them until I sailed
Into the dark of the woods,
Flying always into the moonlight
And out again into rain
That filled my mouth

With a great life-giving word,
And into the many lights
The towns hung up for Christmas
Sales, the berries and tinsel,
And then out again
Into the countryside.
Everyone I passed

Could never believe what they saw,
But gave me one look
They would never forget, as I stood
In my overalls, stretched on the nails,
And went by, or stood
In the steaming night yards,
Waiting to couple on,
Overhanging the cattle coming
Into the cars from the night-lights.
The worst pain was when
We shuddered away from the platforms.
I lifted my head and croaked
Like a crow, and the nails
Vibrated with something like music
Endlessly clicking with movement
And the powerful, simple curves.
I learned where the oil lay
Under the fields,
Where the water ran
With the most industrial power,
Where the best corn would grow
And what manure to use
On any field that I saw.

If riches were there,
Whatever it was would light up
Like a bonfire seen through an eyelid
And begin to be words
That would go with the sound of the rails.
Ghostly bridges sprang up across rivers,
Mills towered where they would be,
Slums tottered, and buildings longed
To bear up their offices.
I hung for years
And in the end knew it all
Through pain: the land,
The future of profits and commerce
And also humility
Without which none of it mattered.
In the stockyards east of Chicago

One evening, the orphans assembled
Like choir boys
And drew the nails from my hands
And from my accustomed feet.
I stumbled with them to their homes
In Hooverville

And began to speak
In a chapel of galvanized tin
Of what one wishes for
When streaming alone into woods
And out into sunlight and moonlight
And when having a station lamp bulb
In one eye and not the other
And under the bites

Of snowflakes and clouds of flies
And the squandered dust of the prairies
That will not settle back
Beneath the crops.
In my head the farms
And industrial sites were burning
To produce.
One night, I addressed the A.A.,
Almost singing,
And in the fiery,
Unconsummated desire

For drink that rose around me
From those mild-mannered men,
I mentioned a place for a shoe store
That I had seen near the yards
As a blackened hulk with potential.
A man rose up,
Took a drink from a secret bottle,
And hurried out of the room.
A year later to the day
He knelt at my feet
In a silver suit of raw silk.
I sang to industrial groups
With a pearl-inlaid guitar

And plucked the breast-straining strings
With a nail that had stood through my hand.
I could not keep silent
About the powers of water,
Or where the coal beds lay quaking,

Or where electrical force
Should stalk in its roofless halls
Alone through the night wood,
Where the bridges should leap,
Striving with all their might
To connect with the other shore
To carry the salesmen.
I gave all I knew
To the owners, and they went to work.
I waked, not buried in pebbles

Behind the tank car,
But in the glimmering steeple
That sprang as I said it would
And lifted the young married couples,
Clutching their credit cards,
Boldly into and out of
Their American lives.
I said to myself that the poor
Would always be poor until
The towers I knew of should rise
And the oil be tapped:
That I had literally sung
My sick country up from its deathbed,
But nothing would do,
No logical right holds the truth.
In the sealed rooms I think of this,
Recording the nursery songs
In a checkered and tailored shirt,

As a guest on TV shows
And in my apartment now:
This is all a thing I began
To believe, to change, and to sell
When I opened my mouth to the rich.

PART THREE

THE BEING

I

It is there, above him, beyond, behind,

Distant, and near where he lies in his sleep
Bound down as for warranted torture.
Through his eyelids he sees it

Drop off its wings or its clothes.
He groans, and breaks almost from

Or into another sleep.
Something fills the bed he has been
Able only to half-fill.

He turns and buries his head.

II

Moving down his back,
Back up his back,
Is an infinite, unworldly frankness,
Showing him what an entire

55

Possession nakedness is.
Something over him

Is praying.
                    It reaches down under
His eyelids and gently lifts them.
He expects to look straight into eyes
And to see thereby through the roof.

                    III
Darkness. The windowpane stirs.
His lids close again, and the room

Begins to breathe on him
As through the eyeholes of a mask.

The praying of prayer
Is not in the words but the breath.

It sees him and touches him
All over, from everywhere.
It lifts him from the mattress
To be able to flow around him

In the heat from a coal bed burning
Far under the earth.
He enters — enters with . . .

What? His tongue? A word?
His own breath? Some part of his body?
All.
                    None.

He lies laughing silently
In the dark of utter delight.

IV

It glides, glides
Lightly over him, over his chest and legs.
All breath is called suddenly back

Out of laughter and weeping at once.
His face liquefies and freezes

Like a mask. He goes rigid
And breaks into sweat from his heart
All over his body

In something's hands.

V

He sleeps, and the windowpane
Ceases to flutter.
Frost crawls down off it
And backs into only
The bottom two corners of glass.

VI

He stirs, with the sun held at him
Out of late-winter dawn, and blazing
Levelly into his face.
He blazes back with his eyes closed,
Given, also, renewed

Fertility, to raise
Dead plants and half-dead beasts

Out of their thawing holes,

And children up,
From mortal women or angels,
As true to themselves as he

Is only in visited darkness
For one night out of the year,

And as he is now, seeing straight
Through the roof, wide, wider,

Wide awake.

BREATH

Breath is on my face when the cloudy sun
    Is on my neck.
By it, the dangers of water are carefully
    Kept; kept back:

This is done with your father again
    In memory, it says.
Let me kneel on the boards of the rowboat,
    Father, where it sways

Among the fins and shovel heads
    Of surfaced sharks
And remember how I saw come shaping up
    Through lightening darks

Of the bay another thing that rose
    From the depths on air
And opened the green of its skull to breathe
    What we breathed there.

A porpoise circled around where I
    Lay in your hands
And felt my fear apportioned to the sharks,
    Which fell to sands

Two hundred feet down within cold.
    Looking over the side,
I saw that beak rise up beneath my face
    And a hole in the head

Open greenly, and then show living pink,
    And breath come out

In a mild, unhurried, unfathomable sigh
        That raised the boat

    And left us all but singing in midair.
        Have you not seen,
Father, in Heaven, the eye of earthly things
        Open and breathe green,

    Bestowing comfort on the mortal soul
        In deadly doubt,
Sustaining the spirit moving on the waters
        In hopeless light?

    We arched and plunged with that beast to land.
        Amazing, that unsealed lung
Come up from the dark; that breath, controlled,
        Greater than song,

    That huge body raised from the sea
        Secretly smiling
And shaped by the air it had carried
        Through the stark sailing

    And changeless ignorance of brutes,
        So that a dream
Began in my closed head, of the curves and rolling
        Powers of seraphim,

    That lift the good man's coffin on their breath
        And bear it up,
A rowboat, from the sons' depleting grief
        That will not stop:

Those that hide within time till the time
    Is wholly right,
Then come to us slowly, out of nowhere and anywhere risen,
    Breathlessly bright.

THE ICE SKIN

All things that go deep enough
Into rain and cold
Take on, before they break down,
A shining in every part.
The necks of slender trees
Reel under it, too much crowned,
Like princes dressing as kings,

And the redwoods let sink their branches
Like arms that try to hold buckets
Filling slowly with diamonds

Until a cannon goes off
Somewhere inside the still trunk
And a limb breaks, just before midnight,
Plunging houses into the darkness
And hands into cupboards, all seeking
Candles, and finding each other.
There is this skin

Always waiting in cold-enough air.
I have seen aircraft, in war,
Squatting on runways,

Dazed with their own enclosed,
Coming-forth, intensified color
As though seen by a child in a poem.
I have felt growing over
Me in the heated death rooms
Of uncles, the ice
Skin, that which the dying

Lose, and we others,
In their thawing presence, take on.
I have felt the heroic glaze

Also, in hospital waiting
Rooms: that masterly shining
And the slow weight that makes you sit
Like an emperor, fallen, becoming
His monument, with the stiff thorns
Of fear upside down on the brow,
An overturned kingdom:

Through the window of ice
I have stared at my son in his cage,
Just born, just born.

I touched the frost of my eyebrows
To the cold he turned to
Blindly, but sensing a thing.
Neither glass nor the jagged
Helm on my forehead would melt.
My son now stands with his head
At my shoulder. I

Stand, stooping more, but the same,
Not knowing whether
I will break before I can feel,

Before I can give up my powers,
Or whether the ice light
In my eyes will ever snap off
Before I die. I am still,

And my son, doing what he was taught,
Listening hard for a buried cannon,
Stands also, calm as glass.

BUMS, ON WAKING

Bums, on waking,
Do not always find themselves
In gutters with water running over their legs
And the pillow of the curbstone
Turning hard as sleep drains from it.
Mostly, they do not know

But hope for where they shall come to.
The opening of the eye is precious,

And the shape of the body also,
Lying as it has fallen,
Disdainfully crumpling earthward
Out of alcohol.
Drunken under their eyelids
Like children sleeping toward Christmas,

They wait for the light to shine
Wherever it may decide.

Often it brings them staring
Through glass in the rich part of town,
Where the forms of humanized wax
Are arrested in midstride
With their heads turned, and dressed
By force. This is ordinary, and has come

To be disappointing.
They expect and hope for

Something totally other:
That while they staggered last night

For hours, they got clear,
Somehow, of the city; that they
Have burst through a hedge, and are lying
In a trampled rose garden,

Pillowed on a bulldog's side,
A watchdog's, whose breathing

Is like the earth's, unforced —
Or that they may, once a year
(Any dawn now), awaken
In church, not on the coffin boards
Of a back pew, or on furnace-room rags,
But on the steps of the altar

Where candles are opening their eyes
With all-seeing light

And the green stained glass of the windows
Falls on them like sanctified leaves.
Who else has quite the same
Commitment to not being sure
What he shall behold, come from sleep —
A child, a policeman, an effigy?

Who else has died and thus risen?
Never knowing how they have got there,

They might just as well have walked
On water, through walls, out of graves,
Through potter's fields and through barns,
Through slums where their stony pillows

Refused to harden, because of
Their hope for this morning's first light,

With water moving over their legs
More like living cover than it is.

GOODBYE TO SERPENTS

Through rain falling on us no faster
Than it runs down the wall we go through,
My son and I shed Paris like a skin
And slip into a cage to say goodbye.
Through a hole in the wall
Of the Jardin des Plantes
We come to go round

The animals for the last time;
Tomorrow we set out for home.
For some reason it is the snakes
To which we seem to owe
The longest farewell of our lives.
These have no bars, but drift
On an island held still by a moat,

Unobstructedly gazing out.
My son will not move from watching
Them through the dust of cold water,
And neither will I, when I realize
That this is my farewell
To Europe also. I begin to look
More intently than I ever have.

In the moat one is easily swimming
Like the essence of swimming itself,
Pure line and confident curve
Requiring no arms or legs.
In a tree, a bush, there is one
Whose body is living there motionless,
Emotionless, with drops running down,

His slack tail holding a small
Growing gem that will not fall.
I can see one's eyes in the brush,
As fixed as a portrait's,
Gazing into, discovering, forgetting
The heart of all rainfall and sorrow.
He licks at the air,

Tasting the carded water
Changed by the leaves of his home.
The rain stops in midair before him
Mesmerized as a bird—
A harmony of drops in which I see
Towers and churches, domes,
Capitals, streets like the shining

Paths of the Jardin des Plantes,
All old, all cold with my gaze
In glittering, unearthly fascination.
I say, "Yes! So I have seen them!
But I have brought also the human,
The presence of self and of love."
Yet it is not so. My son shifts

Uneasily back and away, bored now,
A tourist to the bitter end,
And I know I have not been moved
Enough by the things I have moved through,
And I have seen what I have seen

Unchanged, hypnotized, and perceptive:
The jewelled branches,

The chandeliers, the windows
Made for looking through only when weeping,
The continent hazy with grief,
The water in the air without support
Sustained in the serpent's eye.

IN THE CHILD'S NIGHT

On distant sides of the bed
We lie together in the winter house
Trying to go away.

Something thinks, "You must be made for it,
And tune your quiet body like a fish
To the stars of the Milky Way

To pass into the star-sea, into sleep,
By means of the heart of the current,
The holy secret of flowing."

Yet levels of depth are wrestling
And rising from us; we are still.
The quilt pattern — a child's pink whale —

Has surfaced through ice at midnight
And now is dancing upon
The dead cold and middle of the air

On my son's feet:
His short legs are trampling the bedclothes
Into the darkness above us

Where the chill of consciousness broods
Like a thing of absolute evil.
I rise to do freezing battle

With my bare hands.
I enter the faraway other
Side of the struggling bed

And turn him to face me.
The stitched beast falls, and we
Are sewn warmly into a sea-shroud

It begins to haul through the dark.
Holding my son's
Best kicking foot in my hand,

I begin to move with the moon
As it must have felt when it went
From the sea to dwell in the sky,

As we near the vast beginning,
The unborn stars of the wellhead,
The secret of the game.

APPROACHING PRAYER

A moment tries to come in
Through the windows, when one must go
Beyond what there is in the room,

But it must come straight down.
Lord, it is time,

And I must get up and start
To circle through my father's empty house
Looking for things to put on
Or to strip myself of
So that I can fall to my knees
And produce a word I can't say
Until all my reason is slain.

Here is the gray sweater
My father wore in the cold,
The snapped threads growing all over it
Like his gray body hair.
The spurs of his gamecocks glimmer
Also, in my light, dry hand.
And here is the head of a boar
I once helped to kill with two arrows:

Two things of my father's
Wild, Bible-reading life
And my own best and stillest moment
In a hog's head waiting for glory.

All these I set up in the attic,
The boar's head, gaffs, and the sweater

On a chair, and gaze in the dark
Up into the boar's painted gullet.

Nothing. Perhaps I should feel more foolish,
Even, than this.
I put on the ravelled nerves

And gray hairs of my tall father
In the dry grave growing like fleece,
Strap his bird spurs to my heels
And kneel down under the skylight.
I put on the hollow hog's head
Gazing straight up
With star points in the glass eyes
That would blind anything that looked in

And cause it to utter words.
The night sky fills with a light

Of hunting: with leaves
And sweat and the panting of dogs

Where one tries hard to draw breath,
A single breath, and hold it.
I draw the breath of life
For the dead hog:
I catch it from the still air,
Hold it in the boar's rigid mouth,
And see

A young aging man with a bow
And a green arrow pulled to his cheek
Standing deep in a mountain creek bed,
Stiller than trees or stones,
Waiting and staring

Beasts, angels,
I am nearly that motionless now

There is a frantic leaping at my sides
Of dogs coming out of the water

The moon and the stars do not move

I bare my teeth, and my mouth
Opens, a foot long, popping with tushes

A word goes through my closed lips

I gore a dog, he falls, falls back
Still snapping, turns away and dies
While swimming. I feel each hair on my back
Stand up through the eye of a needle

Where the hair was
On my head stands up
As if it were there

The man is still; he is stiller: still

Yes.

Something comes out of him
Like a shaft of sunlight or starlight.
I go forward toward him

(Beasts, angels)

With light standing through me,
Covered with dogs, but the water
Tilts to the sound of the bowstring

The planets attune all their orbits

The sound from his fingers,
Like a plucked word, quickly pierces
Me again, the trees try to dance
Clumsily out of the wood

I have said something else

And underneath, underwater,
In the creek bed are dancing
The sleepy pebbles

The universe is creaking like boards
Thumping with heartbeats
And bonebeats

And every image of death
In my head turns red with blood.
The man of blood does not move

My father is pale on my body

The dogs of blood
Hang to my ears,
The shadowy bones of the limbs
The sun lays on the water
Mass darkly together

Moonlight, moonlight

The sun mounts my hackles
And I fall; I roll
In the water;
My tongue spills blood
Bound for the ocean;
It moves away, and I see
The trees strain and part, see him
Look upward

Inside the hair helmet
I look upward out of the total
Stillness of killing with arrows.
I have seen the hog see me kill him
And I was as still as I hoped.
I am that still now, and now.
My father's sweater
Swarms over me in the dark.
I see nothing, but for a second

Something goes through me
Like an accident, a negligent glance,

Like the explosion of a star
Six billion light years off
Whose light gives out

Just as it goes straight through me.
The boar's blood is sailing through rivers
Bearing the living image
Of my most murderous stillness.
It picks up speed
And my heart pounds.
The chicken-blood rust at my heels
Freshens, as though near a death wound
Or flight. I nearly lift
From the floor, from my father's grave
Crawling over my chest,

And then get up
In the way I usually do.
I take off the head of the hog
And the gaffs and the panting sweater
And go down the dusty stairs
And never come back.

I don't know quite what has happened
Or that anything has,

Hoping only that
The irrelevancies one thinks of
When trying to pray
Are the prayer,

And that I have got by my own
Means to the hovering place
Where I can say with any
Other than the desert fathers —
Those who saw angels come,
Their body glow shining on bushes
And sheep's wool and animal eyes,
To answer what questions men asked
In Heaven's tongue,
Using images of earth
Almightily:

PROPHECIES, FIRE IN THE SINFUL TOWERS,
WASTE AND FRUITION IN THE LAND,
CORN, LOCUSTS AND ASHES,
THE LION'S SKULL PULSING WITH HONEY,
THE BLOOD OF THE FIRST-BORN,
A GIRL MADE PREGNANT WITH A GLANCE
LIKE AN EXPLODING STAR
AND A CHILD BORN OF UTTER LIGHT —

Where I can say only, and truly,
That my stillness was violent enough,
That my brain had blood enough,
That my right hand was steady enough,
That the warmth of my father's wool grave
Imparted love enough
And the keen heels of feathery slaughter
Provided lift enough,
That reason was dead enough

For something important to be:

That, if not heard,
It may have been somehow said.

PART FOUR

THE DRIVER

At the end of the war I arose
From my bed in the tent and walked
Where the island fell through white stones
Until it became the green sea.
Into light that dazzled my brain
Like the new thought of peace, I walked
Until I was swimming and singing.

Over the foundered landing craft
That took the island, I floated,
And then like a thistle came
On the deep wind of water to rest
Far out, my long legs of shadow down-
pointing to ground where my soul
Could take root and spring as it must.

Below me a rusted halftrack
Moved in the depths with the movement
One sees a thing take through tears
Of joy, or terrible sorrow,

81

A thing which in quietness lies
Beyond both. Slowly I sank
And slid into the driver's shattered seat.

Driving through the country of the drowned
On a sealed, secret-keeping breath,
Ten feet under water, I sat still,
Getting used to the burning stare
Of the wide-eyed dead after battle.
I saw, through the sensitive roof —
The uneasy, lyrical skin that lies

Between death and life, trembling always —
An airplane come over, perfectly
Soundless, but could not tell
Why I lived, or why I was sitting,
With my lungs being shaped like two bells,
At the wheel of a craft in a wave
Of attack that broke upon coral.

"I become pure spirit," I tried
To say, in a bright smoke of bubbles,
But I was becoming no more
Than haunted, for to be so
Is to sink out of sight, and to lose
The power of speech in the presence
Of the dead, with the eyes turning green,

And to leap at last for the sky
Very nearly too late, where another
Leapt and could not break into
His breath, where it lay, in battle

As in peace, available, secret,
Dazzling and huge, filled with sunlight,
For thousands of miles on the water.

HORSES AND PRISONERS

In the war where many men fell
Wind blew in a ring, and was grass.
Many horses fell also to rifles
On a track in the Philippine Islands
And divided their still, wiry meat
To be eaten by prisoners.
I sat at the finish line
At the end of the war

Knowing that I would live.
Long grass went around me, half wind,
Where I rode the rail of the infield
And the dead horses travelled in waves
On past the finishing post.
Dead wind lay down in live grass,
The flowers, pounding like hooves,
Stood up in the sun and were still,

And my mind, like a fence on fire,
Went around those unknown men:
Those who tore from the red, light bones
The intensified meat of hunger
And then lay down open-eyed
In a raw, straining dream of new life.
Joy entered the truth and flowed over
As the wind rose out of the grass

Leaping with red and white flowers:
Joy in the bone-strewn infield
Where clouds of barbed wire contained
Men who ran in a vision of greenness,
Sustained by the death of beasts,

On the tips of the sensitive grass blades,
Each footstep putting forth petals,
Their bones light and strong as the wind.

From the fence I dropped off and waded
Knee-deep in the billowing homestretch
And picked up the red of one flower.
It beat in my hand like my heart,
Filled with the pulse of the air,
And I felt my long thighbones yearn
To leap with the trained, racing dead.
When beasts are fallen in wars

For food, men seeking a reason to live
Stand mired in the on-going grass
And sway there, sweating and thinking,
With fire coming out of their brains
Like the thought of food and life
Of prisoners. When death moves close
In the night, I think I can kill it:
Let a man let his mind burn and change him

To one who was prisoner here
As he sings in his sleep in his home,
His mane streaming over the pillows,
The white threads of time
Mixed with the hair of his temples,
His grave-grass risen without him:
Now, in the green of that sleep,
Let him start the air of the island

From the tangled gate of jute string
That hangs from the battered grandstand
Where hope comes from animal blood
And the hooves of ghosts become flowers
That a captive may run as in Heaven:
Let him strip the dead shirt from his chest
And, sighing like all saved men,
Take his nude child in his arms.

DRINKING FROM A HELMET

I

I climbed out, tired of waiting
For my foxhole to turn in the earth
On its side or its back for a grave,
And got in line
Somewhere in the roaring of dust.
Every tree on the island was nowhere,
Blasted away.

II

In the middle of combat, a graveyard
Was advancing after the troops
With laths and balls of string;
Grass already tinged it with order.
Between the new graves and the foxholes
A green water-truck stalled out.
I moved up on it, behind
The hill that cut off the firing.

III

My turn, and I shoved forward
A helmet I picked from the ground,
Not daring to take mine off
Where somebody else may have come
Loose from the steel of his head.

IV

Keeping the foxhole doubled
In my body and begging
For water, safety, and air,
I drew water out of the truckside
As if dreaming the helmet full.

87

In my hands, the sun
Came on in a feathery light.

V

In midair, water trimming
To my skinny dog-faced look
Showed my life's first all-out beard
Growing wildly, escaping from childhood,
Like the beards of the dead, all now
Underfoot beginning to grow.
Selected ripples wove through it,
Knocked loose with a touch from all sides
Of a brain killed early that morning,
Most likely, and now
In its absence holding
My sealed, sunny image from harm,
Weighing down my hands,
Shipping at the edges,
Too heavy on one side, then the other.

VI

I drank, with the timing of rust.
A vast military wedding
Somewhere advanced one step.

VII

All around, equipment drifting in light,
Men drinking like cattle and bushes,
Cans, leather, canvas and rifles,
Grass pouring down from the sun
And up from the ground.

88

Grass: and the summer advances
Invisibly into the tropics.
Wind, and the summer shivers
Through many men standing or lying
In the GI gardener's hand
Spreading and turning green
All over the hill.

VIII

At the middle of water
Bright circles dawned inward and outward
Like oak rings surviving the tree
As its soul, or like
The concentric gold spirit of time.
I kept trembling forward through something
Just born of me.

IX

My nearly dead power to pray
Like an army increased and assembled,
As when, in a harvest of sparks,
The helmet leapt from the furnace
And clamped itself
On the heads of a billion men.
Some words directed to Heaven
Went through all the strings of the graveyard
Like a message that someone sneaked in,
Tapping a telegraph key
At dead of night, then running
For his life.

X

I swayed, as if kissed in the brain.
Above the shelled palm-stumps I saw
How the tops of huge trees might be moved
In a place in my own country
I never had seen in my life.
In the closed dazzle of my mouth
I fought with a word in the water
To call on the dead to strain
Their muscles to get up and go there.
I felt the difference between
Sweat and tears when they rise,
Both trying to melt the brow down.

On even the first day of death
The dead cannot rise up,
But their last thought hovers somewhere
For whoever finds it.
My uninjured face floated strangely
In the rings of a bodiless tree.
Among them, also, a final
Idea lived, waiting
As in Ariel's limbed, growing jail.

I stood as though I possessed
A cool, trembling man
Exactly my size, swallowed whole.
Leather swung at his waist,
Web-cord, buckles, and metal,
Crouching over the dead

Where they waited for all their hands
To be connected like grass-roots.

XIII

In the brown half-life of my beard
The hair stood up
Like the awed hair lifting the back
Of a dog that has eaten a swan.
Now light like this
Staring into my face
Was the first thing around me at birth.
Be no more killed, it said.

XIV

The wind in the grass
Moved gently in secret flocks,
Then spread to be
Nothing, just where they were.
In delight's
Whole shining condition and risk,
I could see how my body might come
To be imagined by something
That thought of it only for joy.

XV

Fresh sweat and unbearable tears
Drawn up by my feet from the field
Between my eyebrows became
One thing at last,
And I could cry without hiding.
The world dissolved into gold;
I could have stepped up into air.

91

I drank and finished
Like tasting of Heaven,
Which is simply of,
At seventeen years,
Not dying wherever you are.

Enough
Shining, I picked up my carbine and said.
I threw my old helmet down
And put the wet one on.
Warmed water ran over my face.
My last thought changed, and I knew
I inherited one of the dead.

I saw tremendous trees
That would grow on the sun if they could,
Towering. I saw a fence
And two boys facing each other,
Quietly talking,
Looking in at the gigantic redwoods,
The rings in the trunks turning slowly
To raise up stupendous green.
They went away, one turning
The wheels of a blue bicycle,
The smaller one curled catercornered
In the handlebar basket.

XVIII

I would survive and go there,
Stepping off the train in a helmet

That held a man's last thought,
Which showed him his older brother
Showing him trees.
I would ride through all
California upon two wheels
Until I came to the white
Dirt road where they had been,
Hoping to meet his blond brother,
And to walk with him into the wood
Until we were lost,
Then take off the helmet
And tell him where I had stood,
What poured, what spilled, what swallowed:

XIX
And tell him I was the man.

Distinguished contemporary poetry in cloth and paperback editions

ALAN ANSEN: *Disorderly Houses* (1961)

JOHN ASHBERY: *The Tennis Court Oath* (1962)

ROBERT BAGG: *Madonna of the Cello* (1961)

ROBERT BLY: *Silence in the Snowy Fields* (1962)

TURNER CASSITY: *Watchboy, What of the Night?* (1966)

TRAM COMBS: *saint thomas. poems.* (1965)

DONALD DAVIE: *Events and Wisdoms* (1965); *New and Selected Poems* (1961)

JAMES DICKEY: *Buckdancer's Choice* (1965) [National Book Award in Poetry, 1966]; *Drowning With Others* (1962); *Helmets* (1964)

DAVID FERRY: *On the Way to the Island* (1960)

ROBERT FRANCIS: *The Orb Weaver* (1960)

JOHN HAINES: *Winter News* (1966)

RICHARD HOWARD: *The Damages* (1967); *Quantities* (1962)

BARBARA HOWES: *Light and Dark* (1959)

DAVID IGNATOW: *Figures of the Human* (1964); *Rescue the Dead* (1968); *Say Pardon* (1961)

DONALD JUSTICE: *Night Light* (1967); *The Summer Anniversaries* (1960) [A Lamont Poetry Selection]

CHESTER KALLMAN: *Absent and Present* (1963)

PHILIP LEVINE: *Not This Pig* (1968)

LOU LIPSITZ: *Cold Water* (1967)

JOSEPHINE MILES: *Kinds of Affection* (1967)

VASSAR MILLER: *My Bones Being Wiser* (1963); *Wage War on Silence* (1960)

W. R. MOSES: *Identities* (1965)

DONALD PETERSEN: *The Spectral Boy* (1964)

MARGE PIERCY: *Breaking Camp* (1968)

HYAM PLUTZIK: *Apples from Shinar* (1959)

VERN RUTSALA: *The Window* (1964)

HARVEY SHAPIRO: *Battle Report* (1966)

JON SILKIN: *Poems New and Selected* (1966)

LOUIS SIMPSON: *At the End of the Open Road* (1963) [Pulitzer Prize in Poetry, 1964]; *A Dream of Governors* (1959)

JAMES WRIGHT: *The Branch Will Not Break* (1963); *Saint Judas* (1959)